D0577111

Gordon Cooper Branch Library
76 South 4th Street
Carbondale, CO 81623
(970) 963-2889 Fax (970) 963-8573
www.garfieldlibraries.org

IRAN
the people

April Fast

Gordon Cooper Branch Library
76 South 4th Street
Carbondale, CO 81623
(970) 963-2889 Fax (970) 963-8573
www.garfieldlibraries.org

A Bobbie Kalman Book

The Lands, Peoples, and Cultures Series

Crabtree Publishing Company
www.crabtreebooks.com

The Lands, Peoples, and Cultures Series

Created by Bobbie Kalman

Coordinating editor
Ellen Rodger

Project editor
Rachel Eagen

Production coordinator
Rosie Gowsell

Project development, design, editing, and photo editing
First Folio Resource Group, Inc.
Tom Dart
Greg Duhaney
Debbie Smith

Content editing
Joanne Richter

Proofreading
Carolyn Black

Photo research
Maria DeCambra

Consultants
Dr. Mehrangiz Nikou, Dr. Maria O'Shea, Massoume Price

Photographs
Abbas/Magnum Photos: p. 27 (left); AP Photo: p. 12, p. 14; AP Photo/Enric Marti: p. 15 (right), p. 28 (right); AP Photo/Hasan Sarbakhshian: p. 17 (bottom); AP Photo/Sayaad: p. 15 (left); Art Archive/Archaeological Museum Naples/Dagli Orti: p. 7 (right); Art Archive/Dagli Orti: p. 8; Art Directors/Tibor Bognar: p. 4 (right), p. 22 (both); Art Directors/Foto Werbung: p. 6 (left), p. 24 (bottom); Art Directors/Mohsen Rastani: p. 4 (left), p. 19 (right); Art Directors/Chris Rennie: p. 25 (bottom), p. 31; Bettmann/Corbis: p. 13; Bibliothèque Nationale, Paris, France/www.bridgeman.co.uk: p. 9; Corbis: p. 23, p. 27; Mary Kate Denny/Photo Edit: p. 21 (right); W & D Downey: p. 27; /Hulton Archive/ Getty Images: p. 11 (left); Sebnem Eras/Atlas Geographic: p. 21 (left); Henghameh Fahimi/AFP/Getty Images: p. 5 (top), p. 16; Jean Gaumy/Magnum Photos: p. 26 (right); Hulton-Deutsch Collection/Corbis: p. 11 (right); Atta Kenare/AFP/Getty Images: title page; Peter Langer - Associated Media Group: p. 28 (left); Michael Leckel/Reuters/Corbis: p. 17 (top); Yola Monakhov/Getty Images: p. 18; Michael Nicholson/ Corbis: p. 3; Alexis Orand/ Gamma/Ponopresse: p. 5 (bottom); Gianni Dagli Orti/Corbis: p. 6 (right), p. 7 (left); Caroline Penn/ Panos: cover; Eslami Rad/Gamma/Ponopresse: p. 25 (top); José Fuste Raga/AGE/firstlight.ca: p. 24 (top); SEF/Art Resource, NY: p. 10; Kurt Stier/Corbis: p. 20; Keren Su/Corbis: p. 19 (left); Ramin Talaie/Corbis: p. 30 (bottom); Sion Touhig/Corbis Sygma: p. 29 (left); David Turnley/Corbis: p. 30 (top); Peter Turnley/ Corbis: p. 26 (left), p. 29 (right)

Illustrations
Dianne Eastman: icon
David Wysotski, Allure Illustrations: back cover

Cover: Iranian women enjoy sports such as paragliding since the creation of the Women's Sports Organization (WSO) in 1981.

Title page: Iranian soccer fans, draped in their country's flag, cheer on their team at an international competition.

Icon: Images of a Persian king on his throne appear at the head of each section. Scenes such as these were often carved into stone to decorate the walls of ancient palaces.

Back cover: The *gandar*, or Iranian crocodile, grows to be ten to thirteen feet (three to four meters) long. In winter, it floats in rivers or basks in the sun. In summer, it lies in mud that forms at the bottom of rivers that dry out in the heat.

Crabtree Publishing Company
www.crabtreebooks.com   1-800-387-7650

Copyright © **2005 CRABTREE PUBLISHING COMPANY**. All rights reserved. No part of this publication may be reproduced, stored in a retrieval system or transmitted in any form or by any means, electronic, mechanical, photocopying, recording, or otherwise, without the prior written permission of Crabtree Publishing Company. In Canada: We acknowledge the financial support of the Government of Canada through the Book Publishing Industry Development Program (BPIDP) for our publishing activities.

Cataloging-in-Publication-Data
Fast, April, 1968-
    Iran, the people / by April Fast.
        p. cm. -- (Lands, peoples, and cultures)
    Includes index.
    ISBN-13: 978-0-7787-9316-8 (rlb)
    ISBN-10: 0-7787-9316-8 (rlb)
    ISBN-13: 978-0-7787-9684-8 (pbk)
    ISBN-10: 0-7787-9684-1 (pbk)
  1. Iran--Juvenile literature. 2. Iran--Social life and customs--Juvenile literature. I. Title. II. Lands, peoples, and cultures series.
    DS254.75.F37 2005
    955--dc22
                                                2005001077
                                                LC

Published in the United States
PMB 16A
350 Fifth Ave.
Suite 3308
New York, NY
10118

Published in Canada
616 Welland Ave.
St. Catharines
Ontario, Canada
L2M 5V6

Published in the United Kingdom
73 Lime Walk
Headington
Oxford
0X3 7AD
United Kingdom

Published in Australia
386 Mt. Alexander Rd.
Ascot Vale (Melbourne)
V1C 3032

Contents

Salam!

Fishers on the Caspian Sea, in the north, catch the increasingly rare kilka fish. Kilka fish are threatened by comb jellyfish, which eat a lot of plankton, the kilkas' main source of food.

The people who had always lived on the land called their country Iran, which means "country of the Aryan people." Aryans came from Europe and central Asia and settled on the land beginning around 1300 B.C. The country was known as both Persia and Iran for several centuries. Finally, in 1935, the king, Reza Shah, asked that his country be called by its native name, and the world began referring to Persia as Iran.

A deep pride and faith

The people of Iran have a strong sense of pride in their country. This pride, combined with their **Muslim** faith, influences many aspects of their lives, including their family customs, the way they dress, and their traditional greeting of "*Salam*," which means "peace."

The country of Iran is located in southwestern Asia, in a region known as the Middle East. For thousands of years, Iran's diverse landscape has been home to many different groups of people. Some have settled in the mountains that ring the country. Others have built homes on coasts to the north and south. Still others thrive in the vast desert regions of southeastern and northcentral Iran.

Naming Iran

In the 500s B.C., the province of Parsa, now known as Fars, was at the center of a vast **empire**. Greek explorers who landed in Parsa at the time called the region "Persia." For more than 2,000 years, outsiders used "Persia" to refer to the whole country.

A shrine in the northeastern city of Mashhad honors the religious leader, Imam Reza, who died around 818 A.D. Pilgrims visiting the shrine pass by portraits of two recent religious leaders, Ayatollah Seyed Ali Khamenei and Ayatollah Ruhollah Khomeini.

4

Gatherings such as this one are held both to protest government policies and to honor Iranians who make exceptional contributions to the political and cultural life of their country.

The mountainous area of Darakeh, north of Tehran, Iran's capital, is a popular spot for hiking and rock climbing.

The first rulers

As many as 10,000 years ago, peoples from neighboring lands moved to Iran and settled in small villages to farm and raise **livestock**. As these villages grew into towns and cities, the people began to trade goods with one another and with merchants from nearby countries. Trade routes soon crossed the region.

Elamites

The Elamites ruled an area called Elam, in today's southwestern Iran. Their capital city was called Susa. The Elamites first gained power around 2700 B.C. and ruled for much of the next 1,100 years. Then, the Kassites, a people from Iran's Zagros Mountains, invaded the area. Around 1200 B.C., the Elamites again rose to power and established Persia as an important trade center between Afghanistan and Mesopotamia, or present-day Iraq.

Aryan settlers

The Persians and the Medes were both peoples of Aryan **descent** who migrated westward from Russia and Turkestan. By the 800s B.C., the Persians had settled in Elam and Parsa, while the Medes had settled in Media, a land in northwestern Iran. The ancient Medes and Persians were the first peoples to use horse-drawn chariots, which helped them in trade and battle. The Medes were exceptional warriors, with a well-armed and well-organized army. By 705 B.C., they had conquered most of what is now Iran, including Elam.

(above) Artists in ancient times carved scenes into stone, such as this one that shows ancient peoples called the Medes bringing gifts to their king.

(below) The Elamite ziggurat, or pyramid-shaped tower, of Chogha Zanbil was built around 1250 B.C. near Susa. It was dedicated to Inshushinak, Susa's bull-god. The ziggurat originally had five stories, but only three remain.

6

Alexander the Great

By the 300s B.C., the Persian Empire had weakened under poor rulers, and was easily attacked by invaders. Alexander the Great, the leader of the Greek kingdom of Macedonia, gained control of Persia in 330 B.C. and put an end to the Persian Empire. Alexander encouraged other Greeks to move into the region. Greek eventually replaced Aramaic as the official language, and Greek culture, including art and music, flourished. When Alexander the Great died at age 33, one of his army generals, Seleucid, gained control of Persia.

(below) Alexander the Great, shown in this mosaic, defeated Persian king Darius III at the Battle of Issus in 332 B.C. The battle, fought in present-day Turkey, marked the beginning of the end of the Persian Empire.

The Achaemenians

In 550 B.C., the Persian king Cyrus II, of a **dynasty** known as the Achaemenid Dynasty, overthrew the Medes and formed the first Persian Empire. The empire's lands eventually included Egypt, Anatolia, which is present-day Turkey, and Sind, which is present-day Pakistan. Under Achaemenian rule, Aramaic became Persia's official language, and **Zoroastrianism** became the state religion.

(top) Only remains of the Gate of all Nations stand in Persepolis today. Visitors to the ancient Achaemenian capital passed through the gate on the way to the audience hall, where the king received his guests.

The Parthians

In 250 B.C., the Parthian people settled near the Caspian Sea. They are believed to have come from Scythia, an ancient region of present-day Ukraine. The Parthians rebelled against Seleucid's rule and formed the vast Parthian Empire, which spread across the Middle East and southwestern Asia. The Parthians constantly fought against the Romans for this territory. The Romans wanted control of the region so they would have a central location for trade and for launching invasions into bordering lands.

The Sassanians

The Sassanians, a people from Parsa, rose to power in 224 A.D. They restored ancient Persian traditions and rejected Greek culture. They built cities, palaces, and temples, and created great works of art, including glorious battle scenes that were carved into limestone cliffs. They conquered territory in neighboring lands, including Syria and Mesopotamia, and set out in ships across the Persian Gulf to trade with people in Palestine, Arabia, and Egypt, which lay to the west. The mighty Sassanian Dynasty eventually declined because of struggles both among its people and with other groups. It was finally overrun by Arab forces.

The Muslim conquest

The Arab Muslims lived on the Arabian Peninsula, in southwestern Asia. In 636 A.D., Arab armies, spreading their religion across the Middle East, invaded the area controlled by the Sassanians. During the next five years, Arabs conquered all of Iran except the Elburz Mountains in the east and the Caspian coastal plain in the north.

By 651 A.D., the Sassanian Dynasty had collapsed, and the people of Iran began **converting** to **Islam**. Some embraced Islam willingly, but others converted so they could avoid paying a tax called *jizyah*. *Jizyah* was charged to people who followed other religions. For the next two centuries, most of Iran remained part of the Arab Muslim Empire, although the Persian people refused to speak the Arabic language, and tried to keep their culture separate.

In this stone carving, the Zoroastrian god Ahura Mazda gives the royal crown to King Ardashir, the founder of the Sassanian Dynasty.

 # Endings and beginnings

Around 1000 A.D., a group of Turkic peoples from central Asia, known as the Seljuks, began migrating to Iran, conquering rulers and peoples in their path. The Seljuks settled in northwestern Iran, and ruled over most of the country until the early 1200s. Another Turkic group, called the Kharezm-Shah Dynasty, then overthrew the Seljuk Dynasty and took control.

Mongol rule

In 1219, Genghis Khan, a warrior and ruler from Mongolia, led an army of seven hundred thousand soldiers in an attack against Iran. Millions of people were killed, and cities were completely destroyed. When Genghis Khan died in 1227, his grandson Hulagu Khan finished the

takeover. The Mongols soon controlled all of Iran, as well as China and Turkey.

In 1295, Ghazan Khan, Hulagu's great-grandson, began to restore Iran's cities, industries, and culture. He lowered taxes and encouraged the creation of monuments and other works of art. After Ghazan Khan's death, the Mongol Empire broke apart into smaller regions. A different Mongol leader controlled each one.

(top) Genghis Khan, shown in this illustration from a Persian text, established an empire that stretched from the Adriatic Sea in the west to the Pacific coast of China in the east.

The arts developed in Iran under the rule of Shah Abbas, shown on the right of this mural. Artists and craftspeople produced beautiful carpets, rich textiles, elaborate designs, small, detailed illustrations called miniatures, and illuminated manuscripts, which are handwritten books decorated with gold and silver.

The Safavids and Jafari Islam

In the early 1500s, a thirteen-year-old Turkmen named Ismail, who lived in western Iran, conquered the whole country. He took the name Safavid after his ancestor Safi-od-Din, an important religious leader.

Ismail, who was Muslim, decided to make a branch of Islam, called Jafari Shi'i, the official religion. Iran grew rich through trade with other countries, and became a center for **architecture**, poetry, and **philosophy**. When Safavid emperor Shah Abbas, who ruled from 1588 to 1629, died, many people argued over who should lead Iran. With this fighting, along with a decrease in trade, the Safavids declined in power and were replaced by the Qajar Dynasty.

The Qajars and foreign influence

Agha Mohammad Khan was leader of the Qajars, a Turkic tribe from the lands northwest of Iran. In 1794, Khan brought all of Iran under his rule, but his dynasty was threatened in the early 1800s by Russia and Great Britain. Both countries wanted to control trade routes that led through Iran to India. The Qajars fought against these outsiders, but lost much of their territory in two wars.

When Nasir al-Din became king, or shah, in 1848, he gave Great Britain and other foreign countries control over agricultural and mining products, including tobacco and oil. In return, he received large sums of money, most of which he kept for himself. Mozaffar al-Din took the throne next, and continued to allow foreign control in Iran.

The final dynasties

Mozaffar al-Din's rule was marked by serious financial difficulties, with the government spending much more money than it had. As a result, Iran was forced to borrow money from Russia, which demanded more control in Iran in return.

By the early 1900s, Iranians were unhappy with the Qajar shahs, who seemed to give foreign powers too much control. The people wanted to live in an independent country, free from the influence of outsiders. They demanded change.

The Constitutional Revolution

In 1906, after a year of public complaints, Mozaffar al-Din gave in to the people's demands and created a written set of laws called a constitution. People could now elect representatives to a *Majlis*, or house of parliament, to act on their behalf. This limited the power of the shah, who had been the supreme ruler up until then. The next shah, Muhammad Ali, got rid of the *Majlis* in an attempt to take back control. A year later, angry Iranians sent him into **exile**, and his son took over.

Under British rule?

Despite the Iranians' demand for independence, Great Britain controlled territory and oil operations in the south of Iran. Meanwhile, Russia controlled territory in the north. In 1919, Britain presented Iran with a **treaty** that would have

made Iran a British protectorate. This meant that Great Britain would have protected Iran with its military and given Iranians financial aid. In return, Great Britain would have had control over Iran's government, army, transportation, and communications. Before Iran's government could formally approve the agreement, Iranians found out about it and rebelled, fighting to keep their independence. At the last minute, the treaty was laid aside.

Reza Shah Pahlavi

In 1925, the unpopular Qajar Dynasty was overthrown, and General Reza Khan became shah. Reza Khan, who had adopted the family name "Pahlavi," which was the ancient language of the Sassanians, became known as Reza Shah Pahlavi. Pahlavi became the name of his new dynasty.

In an attempt to modernize Iran, Reza Shah, shown on his throne, gave the government, rather than religious courts, the power to make laws.

The Pahlavi era

Reza Shah strengthened Iran's government and began to modernize the country. His plans included improving the **economy** by developing large industries and improving public education and health care. He encouraged people to adopt western ideas, including those of Europe and North America. Even though Reza Shah improved Iran in many ways, he was a harsh ruler. He banned political parties and **censored** the news media to silence anyone who disagreed with his policies. He also forced Iranians to pay high taxes. People became more and more dissatisfied with his leadership.

Into exile

In the 1930s, Reza Shah tried to lessen Great Britain's control of Iran by increasing trade with Germany. This angered Great Britain, which along with the **Soviet Union** and other countries, was fighting against Germany and its **allies** in **World War II**. When Reza Shah refused to lessen Iran's ties with Germany, Great Britain and the Soviet Union invaded Iran and sent Reza Shah into exile.

Mohammad Reza Shah

Great Britain and the Soviet Union allowed Reza Shah's son, Mohammad Reza, to become shah, if he promised to bring back the *Majlis*. This protected their interests, because the *Majlis* would not likely side with Germany. Mohammad Reza Shah did not control the government as firmly as his father had. He allowed the *Majlis* to make its own political decisions, permitted new political parties to be formed, and gave the press greater freedoms.

These greater freedoms did not last. In the early 1950s, Mohammad Reza Shah's supporters overthrew Iran's prime minister, Mohammad Mosaddeq. They, like the shah, disagreed with Mosaddeq's decision to nationalize, or take control of, the country's oil industry. Until then, the oil industry had been mostly owned by foreign oil companies. After the overthrow, Mohammad Reza Shah began to take more power from the people of Iran. He held unfair elections for the position of prime minister. He also formed a secret police that arrested, tortured, and killed those who disagreed with his policies.

Army troops stand outside police headquarters after a failed attempt at removing Mohammad Mosaddeq from power in August 1953. Mohammad Reza Shah fled Iran, but returned within a week, after his supporters successfully overthrew the prime minister.

The White Revolution

Mohammad Reza Shah also made changes that many people liked. In the 1960s, he divided up large areas of land owned by wealthy Iranians, and gave them to smaller farmers. He developed a plan called the White Revolution, which gave workers a share of profits earned by Iranian industries. He improved **literacy** in the countryside and allowed women to vote. Rural areas still suffered, though, as farmers could not afford to buy equipment that their landowners had previously given to them. Many people moved to the cities, but jobs were difficult to find there and the cost of living was high. Crowded slums developed around the cities.

(top) While in exile, Ayatollah Khomeini, shown on the right surrounded by supporters, laid his plans for a new government system that would be run by Shi'i Muslim leaders.

Ayatollah Khomeini

The White Revolution angered Iran's *mullahs*, or religious leaders. Mohammad Reza Shah's government had taken control of land, buildings, and work that the *mullahs* had once overseen, causing them to lose power and income. When the shah began developing close political ties with the United States, Iranians became fearful that Americans would have as much influence in their country as the British and Russians once had.

One *mullah* who spoke out against the shah was Ruhollah Musawi Khomeini. Khomeini held the title of Ayatollah, which meant that he had reached the highest level of religious study. Khomeini's protests resulted in a police attack on the university where he taught. Many people were killed, and Khomeini was sent into exile.

13

Age of revolution

Beginning in February 1978, hundreds of thousands of Iranians, from farmers to city businesspeople, poured into the streets to demand that Mohammad Reza Shah step down. This movement, led by the *mullahs*, became known as the Islamic Revolution.

The rebellion by Iranians caused the shah to give up his power. In January 1979, he and his wife left Iran, never to return. Ayatollah Khomeini returned to Iran and set up his own government council, which began to take power away from the *Majlis*. In an election held in April 1979, most of the country voted in favor of an Islamic republic. Iran became a country ruled by a group of elected and appointed leaders, including a president and vice president,

instead of a shah. Khomeini, as the *faqih*, or supreme religious leader, was the most powerful person in the country. He led a republic guided by the principles of Islam.

The creation of an Islamic republic

The new republic was the world's first and only Shi'i Muslim state. Under the new government, a strict Muslim society developed. Alcohol and most forms of entertainment were banned, and strict Muslim dress codes and behavior were enforced. Some Iranians felt that the return to a more traditional society was a step backward for the country. Many people who had been educated in the West and who had less traditional views, including doctors, teachers, and lawyers, fled Iran.

(top) Iranians burn an effigy, or dummy, representing Mohammad Reza Shah during a demonstration in Tehran.

Crisis at the embassy

In November 1979, Mohammad Reza flew to the United States for medical treatment. The Americans' offer to help him angered many Iranians, who felt that the former shah should be sent back to Iran and stand trial for his violent actions and abuse of power. Iranian students stormed the United States' Embassy in Tehran and took 66 employees hostage. It was not until 444 days later that the last of the captives returned safely to the U.S.

At war with Iraq

In September 1980, Iraq's air force attacked Iran, marking the beginning of the Iran-Iraq War. Iraq wanted to gain complete control of the Shatt al-Arab waterway, which served as a border between the two countries. Iraq also wanted to control the oil fields in western Iran. Finally, Iraq's government, which was ruled by Sunni Muslims, feared that the Shi'i revolution in Iran would encourage the Shi'is in Iraq to rebel against their own government.

The war raged between Iran and Iraq for eight violent years. When the Iran-Iraq War finally ended in 1988, each country had spent $100 billion and lost around 500,000 lives. The fighting destroyed farmland and damaged oil pipelines and trading ports. Entire cities, towns, and villages were wiped out.

The legacy of change

Ayatollah Khomeini died in 1989 and Ayatollah Seyed Ali Khamenei, who had been president since 1981, became *faqih*. In 1997, Mohammad Khatami was elected president. He called for greater freedoms for the Iranian people, and appointed the first female vice president, Massoumeh Ebtekar. He improved trade relations with Europe and Russia, gave the press more freedom, and increased the wages of teachers and other public employees. There are still struggles, however, between groups who support the changes and those who want Iran to follow the Muslim code more strictly.

(above) Mohammad Khatami was originally elected in 1997, then he was reelected in 2001. He won the elections largely because he promised to include all Iranians in the political decision-making process and to improve conditions for women in Iran.

(left) Ayatollah Khomeini encouraged other countries in the Middle East to undergo Islamic revolutions, as Iran had.

15

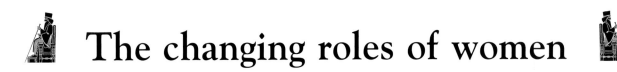

The changing roles of women

Since the 700s A.D., Iranian men and women have followed the Muslim code of behavior. The code is written in the Muslim holy book, the *Qur'an*. The *Qur'an* states that men and women are equal, but that they play different roles in society and have different responsibilities.

Traditionally, Iranian women have been responsible for raising children. Some mothers prepared their daughters for this job by teaching them at home. Many other girls were educated at school and encouraged to work outside the home. When outside, women have often been required to dress according to a custom called *hijab*. *Hijab* is meant to protect a woman's **modesty**. The traditional Iranian *hijab* garment is a *chador*, a long black cloak that covers a woman almost completely from head to toe. A more modern form of *hijab* involves wearing a *magnae*, or scarf, to cover the head, along with a *rouposh*, or long, baggy coat, over pants.

Women in public must follow the custom of hijab. *When at home or in the company of other women, some women still follow* hijab, *while others wear western-style clothing.*

Reforms

After Reza Shah came to power in 1925, he opened non-religious schools, against the wishes of traditional Muslim leaders, and he urged girls to attend. Reza Shah encouraged women to work outside the home, and many women earned positions in government, medicine, law, and business. The shah outlawed the traditional *chador*, as well as other headwear, such as veils and scarfs. The banning of the *chador* upset women from traditional families who felt more comfortable following the custom of *hijab*.

In 1967, Mohammad Reza Shah created the Family Protection Law. This law gave women more rights in the home and workplace. According to one law, a man could no longer divorce his wife without reason, and both husband and wife were required to agree to a divorce. Even though these changes allowed women more freedoms and new opportunities,

many women disliked the harsh way Mohammad Reza Shah enforced the new rules. Some women began to demand the overthrow of Mohammad Reza Shah and supported Ayatollah Khomeini instead. Khomeini said that stricter Muslim rule would restore dignity to women.

Life under the Ayatollah

In 1979, within two weeks of coming to power, Ayatollah Khomeini cancelled the Family Protection Law. He then barred women from becoming court judges, and forced female government employees to follow the custom of *hijab* at their workplace. Within a few years, all women, including foreign visitors, were required to follow *hijab* when in public.

Separating men and women

Men and women were kept separate in all public places because Muslim custom says that there should be no contact between unrelated males and females. Boys and girls were taught at separate schools, except in universities, where men and women sat apart from each other in classrooms. Some Iranians protested against Khomeini's reforms because they were unexpectedly strict. The protests were silenced by Khomeini's government.

Women today

Strict rules still apply to women in Iran today, although the laws and the ways in which they are enforced have changed since Khomeini was in charge. Many Iranian women work in professional fields, such as medicine, education, and filmmaking. Girls and young women attend both religious and non-religious schools and universities. Females over the age of nine must still follow the custom of *hijab* in public, but women, especially in cities, wear jeans beneath their *rouposh*, shorter coats in bright colors and patterns, and colorful scarfs.

The first group of Iranian policewomen graduated from the police academy in Tehran in 2003.

A new generation of Iranian women wants to respect Muslim beliefs, but in a way that is modern and fair to women. They are fighting for fewer restrictions on women's behavior, the return of the Family Protection Law, and equal work opportunities for men and women. Many Iranian women are also pushing for the right to choose whether or not to follow the custom of *hijab*.

In 2003, Shirin Ebadi became the first Muslim woman and the first Iranian to win the Nobel Peace Prize for her work as a human rights activist. Throughout her career as a lawyer, she has fought for the rights of women and children in Iran.

The people of Iran

People of Persian descent make up roughly 50 percent of Iran's population, yet many other ethnic groups, including Azaris, Armenians, Assyrians, and Jews, have settled on the land. Historically, many groups have had little contact with one another because large distances separated them. This has meant that the groups have been able to retain their languages and customs for hundreds, or even thousands, of years.

Persians

Persians are descendants of the first Aryan settlers. They live mostly in the central desert plateau and in Iran's northern provinces. They speak Persian, which they call Farsi, and most are Shi'i Muslims. Their traditional dress varies by region, but men usually wear wide, loose pants, a long tunic, and a cap or large turban. Women's traditional dress includes wide, loose pants, a dress, a veil, and often a shawl.

(top) Today, Persian men usually wear western-style clothing, as do women beneath their rouposh or chador.

Jafari, or Twelver, Shi'i Islam

Muslims believe in one God. "God" in Arabic, the language of the *Qur'an*, is Allah. Muslims also follow the teachings of God's **prophets**, the last of whom was Muhammad. After Muhammad's death in 632 A.D., two main branches of Islam developed: Shi'i and Sunni. The Shi'is believed that the leadership of Islam was passed down to Muhammad's descendants through his cousin and son-in-law, Ali. The Sunnis believed that the true leaders were those elected from among Muhammad's closest followers.

Over the centuries, other differences in beliefs and *Sunna*, or codes of behavior, developed between Shi'is and Sunnis. A branch of Shi'i Islam, called Jafari, or Twelver, Shi'i Islam is based on the belief that Muhammad's twelfth and final descendant, who disappeared in the 800s, never died. Twelver Shi'is believe that he has been in hiding, and will return one day to lead the people. In Iran, at least 90 percent of the population follows Twelver Shi'i Islam.

The Qashqais are a Turkic people who live mostly around the southcentral city of Shiraz. Traditionally nomadic, many Qashqais have now settled in villages and cities.

Azaris

Turkic peoples make up 25 percent of Iran's population. They are descended from Turkic tribes who migrated from central Asia in the 1000s. About 90 percent of Iran's Turkic peoples are Azaris. They speak a Turkic **dialect** called Azari, and almost all are Twelver Shi'i Muslims. Some Azaris live in small villages in the Azerbaijan region, in the Zagros Mountains of northwestern Iran. There, they work as farmers, herders, and traders. Others live in cities, where they own stores and other businesses.

Since Pahlavi rule, Azaris have not been allowed to learn their language in school, though today there are Azari newspapers and radio programs. Some of Iran's Azaris are striving for language rights and for autonomy, or the right to run their local government affairs.

Turkmen

Two percent of Iran's population belongs to a Turkic people known as Turkmen. Most Turkmen live in the north and northeast, near the Republic of Turkmenistan, and speak a language that is also called Turkmen. The majority live in cities, yet rural Turkmen tribes still flourish in Iran. Many rural Turks are known for their great horseback riding skills. They ride Turkmen horses, which are famous for their **endurance**.

Kurds

There are approximately five million Kurds in Iran, making up seven percent of the population. Kurds live along the western border, in the Zagros Mountains, and share a common culture with the Kurds in neighboring Turkey and Iraq. A traditionally nomadic people, some Kurds still live in the countryside where they work as farmers. Most have settled in cities, which have become crowded with **refugees** from neighboring countries. Iranian Kurds speak Kurdish as well as Persian. The majority are Sunni Muslims, but many also practice Sufism, a **mystical** form of Islam.

Iran's Kurds, as well as Kurds in Iraq and Turkey, have been striving for an independent Kurdish state, but the governments in their home countries have not granted it to them.

Some Bandari women cover their faces with masks called negabs *that have openings only for the eyes.*

Arabs

Arabs make up two percent of Iran's population. The majority are Shi'i Muslims, and they speak a dialect of Arabic, in addition to Persian. Most live in the southwestern province of Khuzestan, but Arabs also live on the Persian Gulf islands and along the southern coast. Arabs who live along the coast are known as Bandaris, from the Persian word for "port." Traditional Bandari dress for women consists of loose pants with layers of embroidered or printed loose wraps over top. Traditional Bandari dress for men is a long, sleeveless, white robe called an *abbas*, sandals, and sometimes a turban. In other areas of Iran, Arab men wear floor-length shirt-dresses called *thobes* or *dishdashas*, and loose headscarfs called *gutras*.

Lurs and Bakhtiaris

Most Lurs live in Luristan, in the mountainous region of western Iran. They are traditionally a nomadic people, but many have moved to cities, villages, or small towns. The Bakhtiaris are closely related to the Lurs. Some Bakhtiaris have moved to larger Iranian cities to work in government positions or in the oil and textile industries. About one quarter of Bakhtiaris live a semi-nomadic lifestyle.

Baluchis

The Baluchis live in the southeastern province of Baluchistan. The climate there is very hot and dry, and rain comes in heavy storms that cause floods and **erosion**. The Baluchis are traditionally nomadic, but they are beginning to settle in villages, in homes that are made from mud or stone bricks. There, they raise camels, sheep, and goats. In **oasis** areas, they grow crops, such as oranges, pomegranates, and bananas. Baluchis are also expert carpetmakers and embroiderers. Their weavings and textiles are known for being long lasting.

Nomadic and semi-nomadic peoples live in tents or small huts, which can be easily packed up and transported by pack animals.

Nomadic peoples

Iran's nomadic and semi-nomadic peoples, including Baluchis, Lurs, Bakhtiaris, Kurds, and Qashqais, move from their summer locations, called *yilaqs*, to their winter locations, called *qeshlaqs*, and back every year in search of food and water for their people and herds.

Nomadic peoples have their own systems of rule and, often, more freedoms than other Iranians. This is because the government is so far away that it cannot enforce its laws. Many nomadic women, for example, do not follow the custom of *hijab*, men and women are not separated, and women may even lead tribes.

The independence of nomadic peoples has made them very unpopular with Iranian governments. Some governments have used military power, including armed attacks, to settle nomadic peoples, while others have offered education, health care, work training programs, and land to encourage settlement. Most attempts have resulted in rebellions, because the nomadic groups do not want to give up their traditional lifestyles and independence.

Comings and goings

After the Islamic Revolution in 1979, a steady stream of people left Iran. Most who left disagreed with the new government and wanted greater freedoms than they would have had under traditional Muslim law. Many went to western Europe and the United States, especially California. Others left because they were members of religious minorities, and they feared **persecution** by the government if they stayed in the new Iranian republic.

While many people have left Iran, large groups of people have moved into the country. Thousands of refugees from Afghanistan and Iraq have poured into Iran during recent wars in their countries. Foreign Shi'i Arabs and Kurds, especially, have moved to Iran to escape persecution in their homelands.

This Iranian family, now living in California, still celebrates Nowrouz, *the Persian New Year.* Nowrouz *also marks the beginning of spring.*

GORDON COOPER BRANCH LIBRARY
Carbondale, CO 81623

21

Life in the countryside

Most of Iran's original inhabitants settled in villages around the edge of the central plateau, as close to a water source as possible. Others chose the rugged landscape of the mountains, which protected them from invaders. Still others settled on the **fertile** coastal plains. Today, gravel roads connect many rural villages that were once isolated from one another.

In the village

Mosques, or Muslim places of worship, stand at the center of many Iranian villages, surrounded by a school and shops selling rice, tea, sugar, and other basic supplies. Village homes on the plateau and in the mountains are often made of mud brick, which stays cool in summer and warm in winter. On the Caspian plain, traditional homes are usually built of wood and raised on stilts. This protects them from damage caused by flooding, a result of rising sea levels and plentiful rainfall.

(right) Many people in rural areas make crafts to sell at local shops.

(top) Homes in the northern village of Masuleh cling to the cliffs of the Elburz Mountains. There are no roads for cars in this steep village, but paths for walking are built on the roofs of houses below.

A look inside

People cover the floors in their homes with woolen carpets. Meals are spread out on a cloth on the floor or on a low table with a charcoal burner beneath. The burner, which is sometimes used in homes without electricity, keeps families warm during cooler months. After dinner, families arrange mattresses around the table and charcoal burner like the spokes of a wheel. Then, they cover the table and mattresses with a large woolen quilt to keep the heat from escaping. This arrangement is called *korsi*.

Baths in hammams, *such as this domed-roof* hammam, *were traditionally built partly underground to catch water from* qanats.

The village *hammam,* or bathhouse

Some rural homes do not have running water, but even people who own homes with running water often bathe in village bathhouses called *hammams*. The baths were traditionally filled with water from springs, wells, or underground tunnels called *qanats*. Sometimes, there were two pools of water, one cold and one hot, heated by fires. People paid, usually with food, to use the bathhouse. They also bathed in water they collected from streams, wells, or open water channels that connected to *qanats*. Today, public showers have replaced some village baths. The showers are heated by kerosene or gas.

Going to the doctor

Since the White Revolution, which began in the 1960s, sick people have gone to health houses for treatment. Health houses are run by teams of two *behvarz*, or health-care workers, who have had two years of basic health training. Doctors and nurses work at health centers in larger villages or cities. There is still a shortage of medical staff in rural areas. To attract more doctors and nurses to these areas, Iran offers its medical students free education in exchange for five years of medical service in villages.

Improving life in the countryside

After the Islamic Revolution, the new government focused on improving conditions in rural areas. The Crusade for Reconstruction is a work project that began in 1979. Students from cities volunteered to help harvest, or gather, crops in the countryside. Soon, volunteers began to help villagers build roads, install water pipes, dig **irrigation** canals, bring electricity to villages, and build medical clinics and schools.

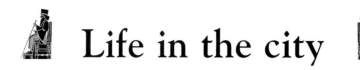

Life in the city

Over the last 20 years, many people have moved from the countryside to Iran's cities in search of work. Housing shortages, traffic, and pollution can be problems in the city, but many Iranians enjoy the benefits of living there. Beautiful old mosques and palaces stand in the heart of historic neighborhoods. Downtown areas bustle with activity, as people go to work or school, shop at bazaars, or attend prayer services at mosques. Office buildings, hotels, restaurants, department stores, and cinemas hum with the rhythms of city life.

Homes

In Iran's cities, neighbors often gather in courtyards with gardens to relax and chat. Newer neighborhoods have houses and apartments made of cement block. In older neighborhoods, homes are often made of mud brick. They are built around closed courtyards, with well-tended gardens and pools. Whether new or old, most Persian homes have handwoven carpets covering the floors.

Mosques decorated with beautiful tilework, temples dedicated to the all-powerful Zoroastrian god Ahura Mazda, and bazaars selling silk and sweets are found in the desert city of Yazd, in central Iran. Yazd is also known for the badgirs, or wind towers, that stand on the roofs of homes, directing cool breezes inside.

A shrine dedicated to the Persian poet Mohammad Shams al-Din Hafiz, who lived in the 1300s, stands in the southcentral city of Shiraz. Hafiz wrote poems about love, religion, and life in Shiraz.

Scooters and motorcycles are convenient ways to get around busy city streets.

At work

The office work week in Iran is five-and-a-half days long, from Saturday to Thursday at noon. The workday includes a two- to four-hour lunch break, which allows Iranians to rest or nap during the hottest time of the day. Many stores are open until 10 p.m., so people can shop when it is cooler. Most businesses are closed on Friday, the Muslim day of prayer.

Bazaars

Bazaars are lively, bustling shopping areas that are set up along narrow streets in almost every Iranian city. Rug merchants, goldsmiths, tailors, food merchants, and metalworkers all sell their wares in bazaars. Shops that sell similar goods are often grouped together. Bargaining, or arguing over the price of an item, is common in bazaars, and allows merchants and customers to decide on a price they both like. The cities of Kerman, Isfahan, and Shiraz are home to some of the finest bazaars in Iran. The bazaar in Kerman is actually many bazaars connected together, some of them between 150 and 700 years old, while parts of the Great Bazaar of Isfahan date back 1,300 years.

A vendor sells pistachio nuts and a sweet called sohan in Qom. Sohan, a Qom specialty, is a flat, sweet biscuit made of pistachio nuts and a flavoring called saffron.

25

School days

Iranian children wait to start the school day. In all elementary and secondary schools, boys and girls study apart, either in different classes at the same school or at different schools.

Throughout Iran's long history, there have been periods when education was mostly religious, and other periods when it was mostly secular, or non-religious. Today, schools follow a secular curriculum, but also offer many religious courses.

Elementary and secondary schools

Iran has both a public school system, partly funded by the government, and a private school system, paid for completely by students' families. In both school systems, students aged six to eleven attend primary school, where they learn math, literature, and science, as well as Islam and Arabic, the language of the *Qur'an*. Then, they spend three years in middle, or "guidance," school. Their marks in middle school determine which program they will follow in high school.

High school lasts for four years. Students attend special programs that prepare them for college, university, or work in a skilled trade, such as carpentry or mechanics.

University

Iran's many colleges and universities offer programs such as teaching, agriculture, medicine, or engineering. Men and women attend the same colleges and universities, but they must sit on opposite sides of the classroom.

Iran also has private religious colleges that are called *madrasahs*. Male students who wish to become *mullahs* must attend these traditional Muslim schools, where they study the *Qur'an* and Muslim law. There are also religious schools for women who wish to lead all-female prayer services. Some students combine a religious education with a secular one. At the Islamic Free University, which has campuses in many cities and villages, students take courses in religion, as well as in literature, medicine, and mathematics.

The largest madrasah in Iran is in Qom. There, men study Muslim religion, law, philosophy, and logic.

Pastimes

Sports

Soccer is the most popular sport in Iran, especially among boys. Another popular sport is *Varzesh-e Pahlavani*, an ancient martial art that began in Iran. It combines gymnastics, feats of strength, and wrestling. It is played in a club called a *zurkhaneh*, meaning "house of strength," where people can watch the participants. Iranians also enjoy watching horse races and playing rugby and football.

Women in sports

The laws of *hijab* have traditionally made it difficult for females to participate in sports, but today, growing numbers of girls and women are pursuing sports such as skiing, cycling, and scuba diving. The Women's Sports Organization (WSO) was created in 1981 to promote women's physical health. It now provides training in sports such as gymnastics, swimming, tennis, volleyball, soccer, and badminton.

Pahlavani wrestlers increase their upper body strength by swinging and throwing heavy wooden clubs, called meels.

Most Iranians enjoy visiting with friends and neighbors, but they have fun in other ways, too. Cities offer a variety of sporting events, restaurants, museums, and poetry readings. Cinemas show films that emphasize Muslim family values, and concert halls host recitals of traditional Iranian and western classical music. Iranians also spend time hiking and picnicking, playing board games such as backgammon and chess, and visiting historical sites and religious **shrines**. Some forms of entertainment, such as popular movies and music, and gambling, are banned because the government considers them to be against Muslim law.

These women dressed modestly in hijab, compete for a spot on the Iranian Olympic archery team. The Iranian Archery Federation held tryout competitions before the 2004 Olympics.

Family customs and celebrations

Iranian families — including grandparents, aunts, uncles, and cousins — spend much of their leisure time together. They also celebrate and mourn together, with religious families following customs outlined in the *Qur'an*.

Birth

A pregnant woman in Iran is treated with special respect. Food is offered to her before anyone else, and she is encouraged to rest and relax. When a woman is ready to give birth, her female relatives all come together to support her. The woman may deliver the baby at home with a midwife, or at a hospital. Female family members attend to the new mother's every need until she is strong enough to care for herself and the child.

In the 1990s, Iran's spiritual leader, Ayatollah Seyed Ali Khamenei, introduced the ceremony of taqlif. Taqlif takes place in all of Iran's girls' schools when girls are nine years old. It marks the time when girls are considered to have reached puberty and must begin to observe the religious duties of Islam.

The *azan*

In traditional Muslim families, when a child is born, the family gathers together, and a male member of the family recites the *azan*, the holy call for prayer. The *azan* states: "God is most great. There is no God but Allah, and Muhammad is God's prophet. Come to prayer, come to security. God is most great." The baby also receives a ceremonial bath, usually on the seventh day after birth for girls and the tenth day after birth for boys.

Marriage

At one time, most Iranian marriages were arranged by the bride's and groom's parents. Marriage was seen as a joining of two families, so parents tried to choose a good match for their children. Today, many young people choose whom they want to marry, but as a sign of respect, they ask for their parents' permission.

A grandfather enjoys time with his young grandchild as they stroll through the streets of Tehran.

The Persian wedding

The Persian wedding ceremony, called the *aghed*, usually takes place at the bride's home or that of a close relative. Traditionally, a *mullah* performed the ceremony, but today many weddings are performed by a qualified government employee.

The wedding reception, called the *arusi*, is held after the ceremony. It is the first of many parties held for the newlyweds over the next few weeks. Guests feast on roasted lamb, sweet rice, stews, pastries, fruit, and an elaborate wedding cake. If the reception is held in a home or private hall, musicians play and dancing continues late into the night. When the reception is over, the bride and groom head to their new home. Before entering, they kick over a bowl of water in the doorway for good luck. In the Zoroastrian tradition, water is a symbol of Anahita, the goddess of **fertility** and birth.

Many young Iranian couples cannot afford to get married, so the government arranges enormous weddings, where hundreds of couples exchange vows at the same time. The ceremony is followed by a party with bands playing folk music and couples receiving gifts that include gold coins and copies of the Qur'an.

Muslims bury people with their heads placed in the direction of the Muslim holy city of Mecca, in Saudi Arabia.

Mourning loved ones

When a Muslim dies, friends and family recite the *Namaz e-meyet*, or prayer of death, so that the deceased may be granted forgiveness from Allah. The body is washed and scented with camphor, the fragrant oil of an Asian evergreen tree. It is then wrapped in a *kafan*, or white cloth, and buried within 24 hours of death.

The *Khatm*, or memorial service, is held on the third day after death. The deceased is further honored on *Hafteh*, one week after death, *Cheleh*, 40 days after death, and *Sal*, one year after death. On these occasions, family and friends visit the gravesite, pray, and gather at home, where foods such as dates, nuts, and sweets are shared. Family members also offer food to the needy as an act of charity, if they can afford to do so.

Yasmin's wedding day

Bridal shops, such as this one in which Yasmin bought her wedding gown, are found in Iran's major cities.

Farah woke up early on her sister Yasmin's wedding day. Farah's mother was already busy, cooking food and decorating their home so that it looked just right.

Farah took special care in getting ready, and put on her loveliest dress. She tucked her hair neatly under her best *magnae*, then joined family and close friends who had gathered in the living room.

At the front of the room, a beautiful, hand-sewn cloth called a *sofreh aghed* was spread on the floor. It glittered with gold and silver threads. Behind it, a mirror reflected two glowing candles. The *sofreh aghed* was covered with fresh flowers, herbs, pastries, candied almonds, sugar cones, a dish of rosewater, and the family's *Qur'an*. Farah's eyes danced at the sight of the beautiful objects before her.

Farah wished she could eat a pastry from the *sofreh aghed*, but she remembered the words her grandmother had told her at her aunt's wedding: "All the items on the *sofreh* are symbols of a rich life for the couple. The sugar represents sweetness. The *Qur'an* represents our Muslim faith at the core of the marriage."

Then, Farah's mother sat beside her. Farah whispered to her, "When will you rub together the sugar cones?"

Farah's cousins buy flowers for Yasmin on their way to the wedding.

Farah's younger sister, Mehri, sits beside Yasmin during the ceremony, carefully watching the bride and groom read from the Qur'an. This is the first wedding Mehri has attended.

"You will soon see," her mother answered.

Before Farah could ask anything more, the bride entered the room, her long, white satin-and-lace gown gliding with her. Yasmin sat facing the mirror, and winked at Farah. A moment later, the groom entered and sat next to her, and the ceremony began.

Farah's aunts stood up and held a large silk scarf over the bride and groom, while the *mullah* recited passages from the *Qur'an*. Farah watched intently as her mother and aunts took turns rubbing the sugar cones together over the scarf, showering the couple with sweetness.

When Farah's mother sat down again, Farah said, "That was my favorite part so far. Now they will have a sweet marriage."

Her mother smiled. "I knew you would like that. Did you also notice the Aunties sewing together a corner of the scarf? That is so that it cannot be broken or separated, as a symbol of Yasmin and Navid's life together."

As the ceremony came to an end, the bride and groom each dipped a finger in a dish of honey and fed it to the other. The honey was another symbol of a sweet life together.

Then, Farah joined her family in offering a gift to her sister. Many relatives presented Yasmin with jewelry or coins. Farah gave her candies and a bouquet of flowers.

Yasmin bent down to hug Farah. "Well, what did you think of the wedding?" she asked.

Farah smiled. "It was beautiful," she answered happily. "But I can't wait for the *arusi* to begin. The pastries and all that sugar have made me hungry!"

Farah's aunts and uncles laughed, and everyone agreed that now was the time to celebrate.

31

Glossary

ally A country that helps another country, especially during a war

architecture The art of designing and constructing buildings

censor To delete or change parts of a book, film, or other publication that are considered offensive

convert To change one's religion, faith, or beliefs

descent Ethnic background

dialect A version of a language spoken in one region

dynasty A family or group of rulers in power for a long time

economy A country's system of organizing and managing its businesses, industries, and money

empire A group of countries or territories under one ruler or government

endurance The ability to withstand repeated hardships

erosion The gradual washing away of soil and rocks, often by rain or wind

exile The forcing of people from their native land, usually for political reasons

fertile Relating to the ability to produce abundant crops or vegetation

fertility The ability to produce children

irrigation A system of supplying land with water

Islam A religion based on the teachings of Allah, the Arabic word for God, and his prophets, the last of whom was Muhammad

literacy The ability to read and write

livestock Farm animals

modesty The state of dressing and acting in a manner that does not seek attention

Muslim Relating to Islam

mystical Having spiritual meaning

oasis Relating to an area in a desert where plants grow because there is water

persecution The act of harming another person for religious, racial, or political reasons

philosophy The study of human beliefs and wisdom

prophet A person believed to deliver messages from God

refugee A person who leaves his or her home or country because of danger

shrine A place dedicated to a holy person

Soviet Union An empire north of Europe and east of Asia, which, when broken up in 1991, was made up of fifteen republics

treaty A formal agreement signed by two or more countries

World War II A war fought by countries around the world from 1939 to 1945

Zoroastrianism A religion developed by the prophet, Zoroaster, based on the belief that a god who represents good continually fights with one who represents evil

Index

1 2 3 4 5 6 7 8 9 0 Printed in the U.S.A. 4 3 2 1 0 9 8 7 6 5